PRIMARY SOURCES

OF

★★★★★★★★★★★★★★★★★★★ ★★★★★★★★★★★★★★★★★★★

IMMIGRATION AND MIGRATION

★ IN AMERICA ★

THE GOLD RUSH

Chinese Immigrants Come to America
(1848–1882)

Jeremy Thornton

The Rosen Publishing Group's

PowerKids Press™
PRIMARY SOURCE

New York

For my brother, Philip Thornton

Published in 2004 by The Rosen Publishing Group, Inc.
29 East 21st Street, New York, NY 10010

First Edition

Editor: Rachel O'Connor
Book Design: Emily Muschinske
Photo Research: Cindy Reiman

Photo Credits: Cover and title page Denver Public Library, Western History Collection, William Henry Jackson, WHJ-10082; cover and title page (bottom right), p. 16 (left) Wells Fargo Bank; p. 4 Hulton/Archive/Getty Images; pp. 7 (right, FN-30892), 12 (FN-01002), 15 (top, FN-04470), 16 (bottom right, FN-02251) California Historical Society; p. 7 (left) © Corbis; p. 8 Hulton-Deutsch Collection/Corbis; p. 11 The Stapleton Collection/ Bridgeman Art Library; pp. 15 (bottom), 19 (left) © Bettmann/Corbis, p. 16 (top right) North Baker Research Library, California Historical Society, FN-32685; p. 19 (right) Courtesy of the Digital and Multimedia Center, Michigan State University; p. 20 California State Railroad Museum.

Thornton, Jeremy, 1973–
The Gold Rush : Chinese immigrants come to America (1848–1882) / Jeremy Thornton.— 1st ed.
    v. cm. — (Primary sources of immigration and migration in America)
Includes bibliographical references and index.
Contents: Chinese immigrants — Gold in California — China hears of the Gold Rush — Gam saan — Chinese migration — Mining camps — Chinese laundries — American citizens discriminate — Developing the West — Anti-immigration laws and beyond.
ISBN 0-8239-6833-2 (lib. bdg.) — ISBN 0-8239-8959-3 (pbk.)
1. Chinese Americans—History—19th century—Juvenile literature. 2. Chinese Americans—Social conditions—19th century—Juvenile literature. 3. Immigrants—United States—History—19th century—Juvenile literature. 4. Chinese Americans—California—History—19th century—Juvenile literature. 5. California—Gold discoveries—Juvenile literature. 6. China—Emigration and immigration—History—19th century—Juvenile literature. 7. United States—Emigration and immigration—History—19th century—Juvenile literature. [1. Chinese Americans—History—19th century. 2. Chinese Americans—Social conditions—19th century. 3. Immigrants—History—19th century. 4. California—Gold discoveries. 5. China—Emigration and immigration—History—19th century. 6. United States—Emigration and immigration—History—19th century.] I. Title. II. Series.
E184.C5 T48 2004
979.4'004951—dc21

2002156302

Manufactured in the United States of America

Contents

Chinese Immigrants

Chinese immigrants were first drawn to America by the California gold rush, which began in 1848. Before then there were very few Chinese in America. By 1852, about 20,000 Chinese had come to find their fortunes in the West. Even after the gold rush, the Chinese kept coming in large numbers. They came to escape a life of poverty in China. They worked hard in all sorts of jobs, and they played a huge role in building up the West. In spite of this, they were discriminated against by American citizens. In 1882, a U.S. law banned the Chinese from immigrating to America. The law was done away with in 1943.

This print from 1877 shows Chinese immigrants arriving in San Francisco. Customs officers are checking the belongings of the immigrants as they leave the ship. The image appeared in Harper's Weekly.

Gold in California

John Sutter, a German-born immigrant, founded what is now Sacramento, California, in 1839. He began building a sawmill in 1847 near the American River. In January 1848, James Marshall, one of Sutter's crew members who was working on the mill, found gold flakes in the river. At first Sutter tried to keep the discovery a secret. He did not want a lot of people coming to look for gold. However, it was not long before word got out and people started to come from all over California and the East Coast of America. After newspapers printed stories about the gold, people came from all over the world, including from China.

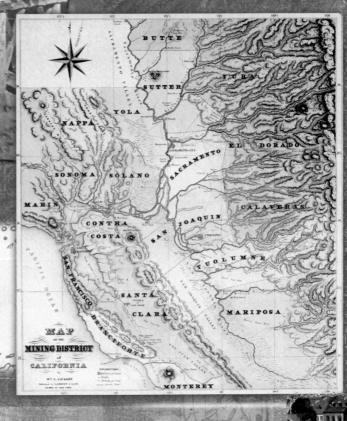

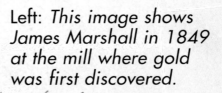

Left: *This image shows James Marshall in 1849 at the mill where gold was first discovered.*

This map of California was made during the gold rush. It shows the locations of towns and gold camps in 1851.

MAP
OF THE
MINING DISTRICT
OF
CALIFORNIA
by
WM A. JACKSON

This photograph of Chinese beggars shows how hard life must have been for many Chinese during the second half of the nineteenth century.

Left: This 1878 drawing by a Chinese artist shows Chinese people dying from hunger.

China Hears of the Gold Rush

At the time when gold was being discovered in the American West, China was experiencing great hardship and poverty. The Chinese government was dishonest and cared little for its people. The Chinese often opposed the government, which resulted in violence and death. Meanwhile, the population in China was growing rapidly, and there was not enough land for everyone. The average family depended on farming to make a living. Many farmers could not grow enough food to feed their growing families on their small pieces of land. When word of the gold in California reached China, many farmers began to send their sons to America. They hoped their sons would send money back to China.

Gam Saan

Chinese ship owners played an important part in encouraging immigration to America. They could make a lot of money bringing passengers there, so they printed advertisements that told of great wealth at Gam Saan, or "gold mountain."

Many Chinese could not pay for the passage to America. Chinese merchants would lend these people money for the journey. Some of the Chinese who borrowed from the merchants paid the money back, with interest, from their earnings in America. Others worked directly for the merchants in America. They worked in groups called tongs in mining or other industries.

This 1842 print shows the terrible living conditions of the Chinese in the port town of Macao in China. A scene such as this helps to explain why so many Chinese people wanted to leave China and go to America.

Chinese Immigration

Some of the Chinese began to immigrate to California as early as 1848, but the larger waves of immigration did not start until the early 1850s. Most of the Chinese emigrants sailed out of the port city of Guangzhou on the southeast coast of China. They sailed on small, crowded ships, and slept below the deck on bunks packed tightly together. The ships also carried goods for sale in California such as tea, silk, and certain kinds of fruit, which were not easy to get in California. The voyage usually took eight weeks. Most Chinese immigrants went to San Francisco, which was the closest port city to where the gold was found.

This 1871 picture by Russell H. Conwell shows groups of Chinese emigrants leaving China for California.

Mining Camps

From San Francisco, the Chinese immigrants went on their search for gold. They set up mining camps by rivers and streams. Usually keeping to themselves, the Chinese miners lived in tents. By the time most of the Chinese came to California, the larger gold pieces in the rivers had already been found by the Americans. It was now harder to find gold. The Chinese miners worked hard, spending long hours in all kinds of weather sifting sand from the riverbeds. Only rarely did they find gold settled on the bottom of their pans. Later, gold had to be mined from the mountains, which was even harder work. Although some of the Chinese did find gold, it soon became clear that they were never going to strike it rich.

Above: This photograph, taken in 1852, shows a Chinese immigrant sifting for gold at Mongolian Flat on the American River.

Right: A Chinese miner carries his tools to a California gold mine.

Right: This engraving shows Chinese immigrants washing and steaming clothes in a laundry.

Above: The Chinese established many businesses in the West, especially in San Francisco. This is a page from an 1878 telephone directory.

Chinese Businesses

By the mid-1850s, the gold rush was finished and gold mining was being done by large companies. The Chinese immigrants could work for these companies or find other jobs. Most found other jobs. The Chinese were willing to work long hours for low pay because they wanted to send money to their families in China. Some cooked in restaurants. Others opened shops or laundries. At the time, American men refused to do laundry. They considered it a woman's job. There were few women in San Francisco, as California was a frontier town and men had settled there first. Chinese laundries were therefore a big success.

Opposite: *After the gold rush, many Chinese settled in San Francisco. The section where many Chinese lived became known as Chinatown. This photograph shows a Chinese man selling lilies in San Francisco's Chinatown.*

American Citizens Discriminate

At the start of the gold rush, the American miners did not mind sharing in the good fortune. They thought that there was plenty of gold for everyone. However, as more immigrants began arriving from all over the world, the competition for gold increased. The American miners who did not find gold grew frustrated. They took their frustration out on many of the immigrants, including the Chinese, and began to discriminate against them. In 1850, the government in California passed the Foreign Miners' Tax, which required each foreign miner to pay $20 per month to the state. Although some of the Chinese paid the tax and continued to look for gold, most felt there was not enough gold to make it worth their while.

Right: *This document was created to tell states outside of California why the Chinese should be kept out of America.*

AN ADDRESS

TO THE PEOPLE OF THE UNITED STATES UPON THE EVILS OF CHINESE IMMIGRATION.

Left: *This print shows the anti-Chinese riot that took place in Denver on October 31, 1880. Angry crowds attack the Chinese and the buildings in which they live.*

Above: Chinese workers are loading 30-foot (9.1-m) lengths of rail onto a push car on the Central Pacific Railroad, about 230 miles (370.2 km) from Sacramento.

Chinese workers drill and split rock. This was one of the most dangerous jobs on the Central Pacific Railroad.

Developing the West

Chinese immigrants continued to come to America after the gold rush. They came looking for work. Many found jobs building the Central Pacific Railroad. The railroad started in California and continued east over the Sierra Nevada. In 1869, it connected with the Union Pacific Railroad at Promontory, Utah. This was the first railroad to cross America. The Chinese immigrants worked hard to build the railroad. The work was dangerous. Many Chinese workers died from accidents caused by the dynamite used to blast through rock. In spite of their hard work, they were paid less than the Americans who worked with them. The Chinese were not recognized for their part in the building of this historic railroad.

Anti-Immigration Laws and Beyond

In the late 1870s, California was going through an economic depression. Many Californians were out of work. Once again they took their anger out on the Chinese, whom they accused of taking their jobs. In 1882, Congress passed a law banning the immigration of Chinese people. The law was finally done away with in 1943.

The Chinese first left China to escape hardship only to find a different kind of hardship in America. Hardworking and patient, these Chinese immigrants managed to make a life for themselves in America. After many years, Americans have finally begun to recognize the contributions that the Chinese immigrants have made to the growth of the United States.